12345
1098 76
12345

6 7 8 9 10

5 4 3 2 1

6 7 8 9 10

First published 1986 by Walker Books Ltd
87 Vauxhall Walk, London SE11 5HJ

This edition produced 2000 for
The Book People Ltd, Hall Wood Avenue
Haydock, St Helens WA11 9UL

Printed in Hong Kong

ISBN 0-7445-0643-3

123

SARA LYNN

TED SMART

one

cockerel

two

horses

three

COWS

four

pigs

five

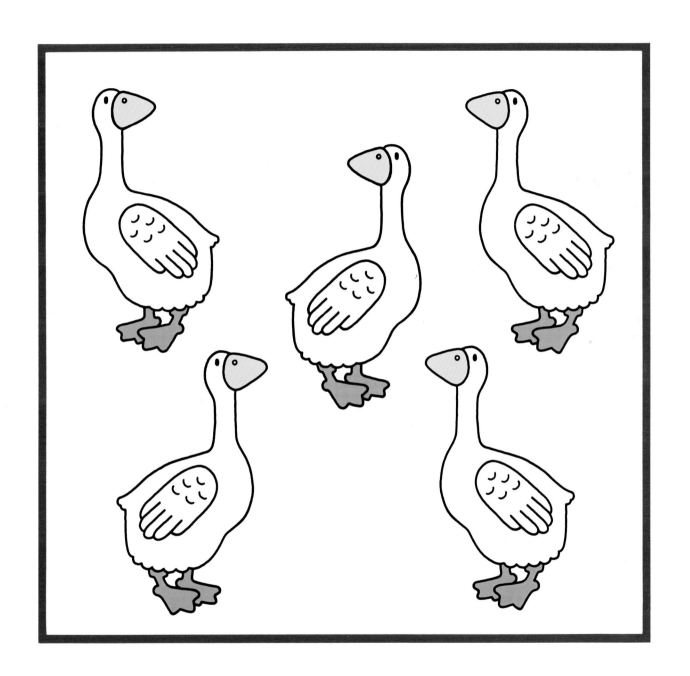

geese

six

sheep

seven

ducks

eight

hens

nine

rabbits

ten

chicks

ten   nine   eight   seven   six

10   9   8   7   6

five 5 four 4 three 3 two 2 one 1

How many of each sort of animal can you find?

one   cockerel

two   horses

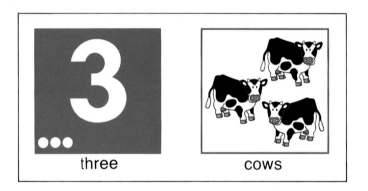

three   cows

four   pigs

five   geese

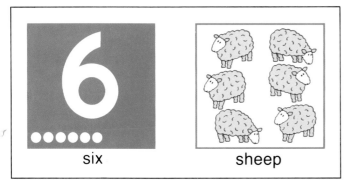

six · sheep

seven · ducks

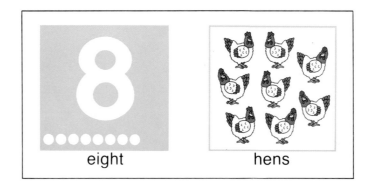

eight · hens

nine · rabbits

ten · chicks